He is Risen!
The Story of Easter
Children's Jesus Book

BABY PROFESSOR
EDUCATION KIDS

Speedy Publishing LLC

40 E. Main St. #1156

Newark, DE 19711

www.speedypublishing.com

Copyright 2016

What do you know of the Easter Story?

God so loved the world that He gave us His only begotten son... He is Jesus. Do you know him? What do you know about Him?

Jesus Christ Our Savior. He is present everywhere for He reigns in our hearts.

In this book, you will know more about Jesus, our Savior, and His death and resurrection. Christians celebrate the resurrection of the Lord, Jesus Christ. They do it on Easter Sunday.

It is one of the big annual celebrations for Christian churches. It marks the end of Lent and the start of the Easter Season.

According to Scripture, on the Sunday three days after Jesus died on the cross, he came back to life and was raised from the dead. Christians hold onto this event as a sign of God's promise of eternal life to them.

Jesus is God's only son. He lived with us to show us how God loves us. Jesus feels our worries and sadness for He was once human like us. He came to redeem us from our sins.

The death of Jesus Christ by crucifixion is well-remembered on Good Friday. This is part of Holy Week, which starts with Palm Sunday and ends the night before Easter.

Jesus' death ends the power of sin and death to rule us. That's how He loves us as children of God.

When Is Easter Season?

Easter Season is in the spring, and its start date changes from year to year. To prepare for Easter, people observe Lent, which involves 40 days of fasting, repentance and spiritual reflection.

The beginning of Lent, as observed in Western Christianity, is Ash Wednesday.

What is Lent?

Lent is the season of preparation before Easter. It is the time to reflect on the life of Jesus Christ, and on how we are living our lives. Christians reflect on the message of hope, and the sufferings and sacrifices, of Jesus Christ. They think about His death, burial and resurrection.

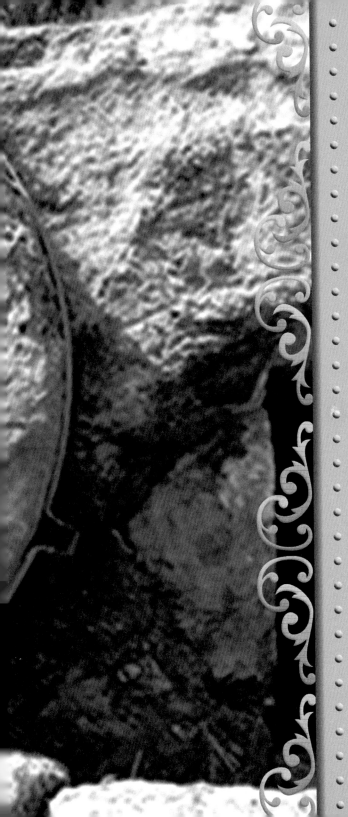

The Story of the Resurrection of Jesus

Jesus' body was placed in His tomb after He was crucified and died on a Friday. Then the tomb was sealed with a large stone. Soldiers guarded the tomb of Jesus.

On the third day, Sunday, several women visited the tomb. They were Mary Magdalene, Mary the mother of James, Joanna and Salome. They were there at dawn to anoint the body of Jesus.

But before they came in the tomb, an angel came from heaven and rolled back the stone. As it was done a strong earthquake happened which scared the guards. When the women came close, the angel, dressed in white, was sitting upon the stone.

The angel then announced to the women that Jesus was no longer in the tomb. The angel said that Christ had risen from the dead, just as He had said he would. To prove that the angel was telling the truth, the women went into the tomb and see for themselves that Jesus' body was no longer there.

The angel told the women to tell the news to the disciples. Immediately, with mixed emotions of fear and joy, the women ran to obey the angel's command. But to their surprise, Jesus met them on their way. When this happened, the women knelt and worshiped Him.

Then Jesus told the women
not to be afraid and to
tell His brothers to go to
Galilee for they would see
Him there. The guards
immediately reported what
had happened to the chief
priests.

However, the priests gave the soldiers a large sum of money so they would keep what they had seen to themselves and not tell anyone about it. The chief priests instructed the guards to lie and to tell the people that the disciples had stolen Jesus' body.

Near the tomb, Jesus appeared to the women after His resurrection. He also appeared twice to His disciples and ate a meal with two of them. Jesus also appeared at the Sea of Galilee and told his disciples to share his good news with the whole world.

Did you enjoy reading?
Don't forget to share this to
your friends!

Visit

BABY PROFESSOR
EDUCATION KIDS

www.BabyProfessorBooks.com

to download Free Baby Professor eBooks
and view our catalog of new and exciting
Children's Books

84946670R00024

Made in the USA
Lexington, KY
26 March 2018